Podcast Starter Pack

Record, Launch & Promote Your First Show on Any Budget
By Mason Wells

Table of Contents

Introduction

Everyone's got something to say.

But most people never hit record.

Why? Because podcasting seems complicated—like you need a studio, a $500 mic, or an audio engineering degree.

You don't.

You can start a podcast today with a phone, an idea, and the right strategy.

You can grow it with time, tools, and consistency.

This book was written for people who:

• Want to start now, not someday

• Don't want to overspend on tech they don't need yet • Would rather create than overthink • Want to eventually scale, grow, or monetize—but without burnout

I'll walk you through every step, from recording your first episode to choosing a podcast host, upgrading your setup, and sharing your show with the world.

You don't have to be famous. You don't have to be perfect.

You just have to start.

Let's get into it.

Chapter 1: Why Podcasting Still Works (and Why It's Not Too Late)

Let's get one thing out of the way:

It's not too late.

Yes, there are a lot of podcasts. But most of them... don't last.

The average podcast dies after just 7 episodes.

Why? Because people overcomplicate it or don't know what they're doing.

That's why this book exists.

——

Why Podcasting Still Works

• It builds connection — people hear your voice, tone, energy • It fits busy lives — people listen while driving, working, walking • It creates trust — more than blogs, videos, or social posts • It's open — you don't need permission or a platform to get started • It's long-game content — episodes live forever

And here's the big one:

You don't need a huge audience to make it worth it.

If 50 people listen, that's like speaking to a full classroom every week. That's powerful.

——

Common Podcasting Myths (That Stop People From Starting)

Myth #1: "I need a great mic first."

Nope. You need good content, not expensive gear. Your phone mic + quiet room = enough to start.

Myth #2: "I need a co-host."

You can go solo, interview guests, or mix formats. You don't need anyone's permission.

Myth #3: "It's too saturated."

Saturated doesn't mean worthless. It means validated. It's a proven channel—now it's about how you show up.

———

What This Book Will Help You Do

By the end of this guide, you'll know how to:

• Pick a podcast format that fits your style • Record your first episode with zero stress • Upload and publish it with free or cheap tools • Promote your show without feeling spammy • Upgrade your setup without breaking the bank

Let's get practical in Chapter 2—where we plan your podcast the smart way.

Chapter 2: Plan the Podcast (So You Don't Burn Out by Episode 3)

Before you hit record, you need a framework.

That doesn't mean scripting every word or having a five-year roadmap. It just means answering a few key questions—so you know where you're going, and why you're doing it.

Here's how to build a podcast you'll actually stick with.

————

1. What's Your Podcast About (And Who's It For)?

Don't overthink your niche—but don't skip it either.

Ask yourself:

• What do I actually enjoy talking about?

• What do people ask me about or come to me for?

• Who do I want to help, entertain, or teach?

Examples:

• "I want to help other freelance writers land better clients."

• "I want to talk about personal finance without sounding boring."

• "I want to tell wild true stories from my job as a bartender."

Clarity helps you show up consistently.

It also helps listeners know exactly why they're pressing play.

————

2. Pick a Format You Can Stick With

Here are common formats—pick one or mix a couple:

Format	Description
Solo	You talk directly to the listener (narrative, advice, updates)
Interview	You bring on guests—experts, creators, storytellers
Panel/Co-Host	Multiple voices, discussions, banter
Hybrid	Mix of solo, interviews, and storytelling

Pro tip: Start solo or with remote interviews (we'll cover tools later). It's less pressure, easier to schedule, and still sounds great.

---

3. Episode Length & Schedule

Don't let this stress you out. You can experiment.

But here's the rule:

Pick something sustainable.

Type	Ideal Length	Notes
Short-form	10–15 mins	Tips, stories, solo updates
Mid-range	20–30 mins	Most common format
Long-form	45+ mins	Deep dives, interviews, storytelling

Start with 1 episode a week if you can. That's consistent enough to build trust, without burning out.

―――

4. Name & Branding

Your name doesn't have to be perfect. But it should:

• Be easy to say and spell

• Hint at the topic or vibe

• Feel natural when said aloud ("Welcome to...")

Examples:

• Creative Control (for content strategy) • Money Talks Unfiltered (personal finance) • The Quiet Hustle (slow-growth entrepreneurship) • Tap In (wellness, spiritual, or mindfulness themes)

Once you've got the name:

• Use Canva to make a cover art (1600x1600 px works) • Keep it readable, simple, and bold—even at small sizes

―――

5. Create a Simple Episode Structure

You don't need a full script—but having a flow helps.

Sample outline:

1. Quick intro ("Welcome back, this is episode 3...") 2. Main topic or interview 3. Call to action (rate, follow, share, etc.) 4. Short outro music or sign-off

Having a loose format makes it easier to create consistently—and helps your listeners feel grounded.

———

Up next in Chapter 3:

What Gear You Actually Need (from $0 to Pro-Level Options)

We'll cover:

• Recording on your phone

• Mics under $50

• Software that makes editing easy

• The gear you can skip (for now)

Chapter 3: What Gear You Actually Need (from $0 to Pro-Level Options)

Here's the truth:

Most new podcasters overthink gear.

They spend more time watching mic reviews on YouTube than actually recording.

Let's fix that.

This chapter gives you three setups:

• No budget

• Small budget

• Step-up setup for later

———

1. $0 Setup — Just Your Phone

If you have a smartphone, you're already good to go.

How to do it:

• Use your phone's built-in Voice Memos or voice recorder • Find a quiet room—car with the engine off, closet with clothes, small bedroom with soft surfaces • Record short test clips to get a feel for your tone and pacing

Optional free apps:

• BandLab (iOS/Android) – free audio editor • Anchor (now Spotify for Podcasters) – record, edit, and publish in one app

Is this the best audio ever? No.

But is it good enough to start with confidence? Absolutely.

----

2. $50–$100 Budget — Entry-Level Mic Setup

If you're ready to invest a bit for cleaner audio, here's what to buy first:

Recommended USB Mics:

• Samsung Q2U – around $70, solid beginner mic • Fifine K669 – around $35–$45, great sound for the price • Blue Snowball iCE – ~$50, decent but bulky

Why USB?

It plugs directly into your laptop—no interface needed.

Also helpful:

• Foam pop filter or windscreen ($10–15) • Mic stand or boom arm (many mics come with one)

Pair this with free software like:

• Audacity (Windows/Mac) – simple, reliable audio editor • GarageBand (Mac) – good for intros, music, and editing multiple tracks • Descript – transcribes and edits by text, great for beginners (free tier available)

3. Step-Up Setup — When You're Ready

If your podcast is growing or you want to level up, here's a step-up gear list:

• Audio Interface – like Focusrite Scarlett Solo ($120) • XLR Mic – like the Rode PodMic or Audio-Technica AT2020 ($100–120) • Boom Arm + Shock Mount – for comfort and cleaner sound • Cloudlifter (optional) – if you use a gain-hungry mic like the Shure SM7B

But none of this is required to start.

Don't let gear become the excuse not to publish.

———

What You Don't Need (Yet)

• A soundproof booth

• A $400 condenser mic

• Complex DAW software like Pro Tools

• An external mixer or multi-track recorder

You can always grow into more gear.

But most of the best podcasts today?

Still recorded on modest setups.

———

Coming up in Chapter 4 – Recording Your First Episode (Without Overthinking It)

We'll walk through:

• Prepping what to say

• Getting your room ready

• Recording in one shot

• Fixing minor mistakes without editing for hours

Chapter 4: Recording Your First Episode (Without Overthinking It)

You've got your idea.

You've picked your gear.

Now... time to press record.

But don't worry—we're keeping this low-pressure and doable.

The goal here isn't to create a masterpiece. It's to create momentum.

----

1. Start with a Soft Launch Mindset

You're not announcing to the world. You're not going viral.

You're simply recording Episode 1.

So treat it like a soft launch:

• This is a test run

• You're learning the process

• You'll improve each time

And remember: You can re-record or replace your first few episodes anytime.

----

2. What to Say in Episode 1

Here's a classic, simple Episode 1 format:

1. Who you are

2. What the podcast is about

3. Why you started it

4. What people can expect moving forward 5. Optional: ask them to follow/subscribe/rate

Example:

"Hey, I'm Mason Wells. Welcome to the very first episode of Podcast Starter Pack. This show is for anyone who's ever wanted to launch a podcast without expensive gear or complicated setups…"

Keep it under 10–15 minutes.

Keep it honest.

Keep it you.

————

3. Prepare a Loose Outline

Write a few bullet points—not a full script.

This helps keep your delivery natural.

A good outline might look like:

• Intro

• Why I'm starting this podcast

• What topics I'll cover

- How often new episodes will drop

- What I hope people get from it

- Quick sign-off

If you mess up—pause, breathe, and keep going. You can edit later.

———

4. Room Setup Tips

Even basic mics sound better when the room is right:

• Record in a small space with soft surfaces (bedroom, closet, car) • Avoid big empty rooms and hard walls • Turn off fans, AC units, loud fridges, or other noise • Put your phone on airplane mode (if using it to record)

———

5. Recording Tips for a Smooth First Take • Sit or stand comfortably • Speak a little slower than usual • Smile when you talk—it really does come through in your tone • Don't stress every "uh" or pause—you're human • End strong, even if it feels awkward

Remember, you're not trying to sound like a radio host.

You're just connecting with people.

———

6. Optional Editing (But Keep It Light)

If you're editing, keep it simple:

• Trim the beginning and end

• Cut out any long pauses or clear mistakes • Add intro/outro music if you have it (free sites: Pixabay Music, Uppbeat)

Don't edit out every breath or imperfection.

Your voice is supposed to sound real.

——

Next up:

Chapter 5 – Publishing Your Podcast (Platforms, Hosts & First Listeners)

We'll cover:

• Where to upload your episodes

• Free vs paid hosting options

• Getting listed on Spotify, Apple, etc.

• How to get your first real listeners

Chapter 5: Publishing Your Podcast (Platforms, Hosts & First Listeners)

Recording your first episode is a huge step.

But now it's time to share it.

This chapter walks you through:

• Choosing a podcast host

• Submitting to platforms like Spotify and Apple • Launching your first few episodes • Getting those crucial first listeners

Let's go.

———

1. What Is a Podcast Host (And Why You Need One)?

A podcast host is where your audio files live.

They generate something called an RSS feed—that's what connects your show to Spotify, Apple, and everywhere else.

Think of it like this:

• You upload to the host

• The host distributes to platforms

• Listeners stream or download episodes through those platforms

———

2. Free & Paid Podcast Hosts

Here are some beginner-friendly hosting options:

Free Options

• Spotify for Podcasters (formerly Anchor) • Easiest for beginners • Free hosting, unlimited episodes • Direct integration with Spotify • Built-in basic editing tools • Auto-distributes to most major platforms • Podbean (Free Plan) • Limited storage (5 hours/month) • Clean interface, good for testing the waters

Paid Options (When You're Ready)

• Buzzsprout – $12–24/mo, super user-friendly, detailed analytics • Captivate – $19/mo, good for growing and monetizing • Transistor – $19/mo, great for managing multiple shows or brands

Start free. Upgrade if you grow.

----

3. How to Submit to Major Platforms

Once your show is live on your host, you can submit to other platforms using your RSS feed.

Here's where you want to be:

Platform	How to Submit
Spotify	Auto-listed via Spotify for Podcasters
Apple Podcasts	Submit via Apple Podcasts Connect (free Apple ID required)
Google Podcasts	Submit via Google Podcasts Manager (Note: Google Podcasts is transitioning into YouTube Music)
Amazon Music	Submit at Amazon Music for Podcasters
iHeartRadio, TuneIn, Pandora	Submit individually or through your host (Buzzsprout and Captivate offer 1-click submissions

It may take 1–5 days to appear on some platforms. That's normal.

———

4. Launch with More Than One Episode

Don't launch with just one.

Drop 2–3 episodes at once so new listeners can binge a little and get a feel for your style.

Then follow up with a consistent release schedule—weekly is ideal.

———

5. Your First Listeners (How to Get Them)

Some quick ways to attract your early audience:

• Share a simple link – Hosts like Spotify for Podcasters give you a free link that works on all platforms • Post on social – Twitter/X, Instagram, Reddit (in relevant communities), Threads, Facebook groups • Ask for support – Tell friends, "Hey, it would mean a lot if you'd listen and rate my new show."

• Use your email signature – Add a link to your podcast in every email • List on directories – Podcast Addict, Listen Notes, Podchaser, etc. (takes 5 minutes each)

You don't need 10,000 followers.

You need a few listeners who actually care—and will tell others.

———

Coming up next:

Chapter 6 – Promoting Your Podcast (Without Feeling Spammy)

We'll cover:

• Social strategies that feel natural

• Building in public

• Promo tools & repurposing

• When (and if) to think about ads or monetization

Chapter 6: Promoting Your Podcast (Without Feeling Spammy)

Most new podcasters hit "publish" and then... nothing.

No clicks. No listeners. No feedback.

Why?

Because they don't know how to promote without being salesy—or they just feel awkward talking about their own thing.

Let's fix that.

Here's how to promote your podcast consistently and naturally, even if you're not a marketer.

_____

1. Focus on One Platform at First

Pick one place to show up regularly.

Could be:

• Instagram

• Twitter/X

• TikTok

• Threads

• LinkedIn (if it fits your topic)

• Reddit (community-focused, but powerful) • YouTube Shorts (even audio + static image can work)

Tip: Go where your ideal listener already spends time—not where you feel you should be.

_____

2. Create Simple Promo Content That Doesn't Suck

Don't just post "New episode out now!" every week.

Give people a reason to click.

Here are 5 types of content that work:

• Audiograms – Short 30–60 sec audio clips with captions (tools: Headliner, Wavve) • Quote graphics – A powerful line from your episode on a clean image • Behind the scenes – A photo or clip of your setup, bloopers, or planning process • Mini threads or posts – "3 things I learned from this week's podcast..."

• Episode takeaways – Give the value first, then link to the full show

Your goal: make it feel shareable, not just promotional.

_____

3. Repurpose, Don't Reinvent

You don't have to make 10 pieces of content from scratch.

Just repurpose the episode.

Example:

• Pull 1 quote → turn into a graphic

• Pull 1 tip → turn into a tweet

• Pull 30 seconds → turn into an audiogram • Write a 3-line caption → post on 3 platforms

You made the episode—let it work for you.

———

4. Collaborate Early (Even If You're Small)

Guests are the #1 growth hack for early podcasts.

Even micro-guests (friends, niche creators, community members) will:

• Share the episode

• Introduce you to their audience

• Help you build podcasting confidence

You can also do guest swaps:

• You appear on their pod

• They appear on yours

• Or just shout each other out

This builds your network and boosts your visibility—fast.

———

5. Ask for the Follow, Review, or Share (But Make It Easy)

At the end of each episode, add a quick, natural CTA:

"If this helped you out, take 10 seconds to follow the show or send it to one friend—it really helps."

Keep it honest. No pressure. No begging.

———

6. Optional Tools That Help

• Headliner – For audiograms and clips

• Canva – For quote graphics and promo images • Podpage – Build a simple website for your podcast • Linktree / Beacons – For an all-in-one link in your bio • Notion / Trello – Plan episodes and track content ideas

———

Bottom Line

Don't burn yourself out trying to "go viral."

Just keep showing up. Keep creating. Keep sharing.

Consistency grows your podcast way faster than perfection ever will.

———

Next up:

Chapter 7 – Upgrading Your Show (When You're Ready to Level Up)

We'll cover:

- When to invest in better gear

- How to create intro/outro music

- Editing tools that save time

- Monetization options when you're ready to earn

Chapter 7: Upgrading Your Show (When You're Ready to Level Up)

You've got a few episodes under your belt.

You're more confident on the mic.

Now it's time to upgrade—without overhauling everything.

This chapter covers the most useful (and cost-effective) ways to level up your podcast when you're ready.

----

1. Invest in Cleaner Sound (Without Going Broke)

If your early episodes were recorded on your phone or a basic mic, now's a good time to upgrade.

Recommended Setup

• Mic: Samson Q2U or Audio-Technica ATR2100x (USB/XLR combo, ~$70–$100) • Pop filter: Reduces breath sounds and plosives (~$10) • Boom arm: Holds mic steady and reduces handling noise (~$20–$30) • Recording space: Add blankets, foam panels, or record in a closet for better soundproofing

Even a small setup upgrade makes your show sound way more professional.

----

2. Add Intro & Outro Music

Adding music gives your show a vibe—and makes it feel more polished.

Where to get free or low-cost music:

• Pixabay Music – Free, royalty-free

• Uppbeat.io – Free tier with attribution • PremiumBeat / AudioJungle – Paid options for exclusive use

Make sure:

• It matches your tone (no EDM intros for a calm mindfulness pod) • It's under 15 seconds • You fade it in/out cleanly with your voice

Tip: Record a reusable intro like:

"Welcome to [Podcast Name], where each week we [promise/value]. I'm your host, [Name]—let's get into it."

———

3. Learn Light Editing (or Outsource It)

At this stage, it's worth cleaning up your audio just a bit more.

Free or beginner-friendly tools:

• Audacity – Still a solid choice

• Descript – Edit your episode like a Google Doc (transcription-based) • GarageBand – Great if you're on Mac

Or, if you want to save time and you've got a little budget:

• Hire a freelancer on Fiverr or Upwork

• Ask for simple cleanup: remove background noise, fix volume, trim pauses

———

4. Monetization Options (No Sponsor Needed)

You don't need 10,000 downloads to start earning. Here are beginner-friendly monetization options:

A. Affiliate Links

Mention tools, books, or products and drop a link in your show notes.

Sites to try:

• Amazon Associates

• Podcorn (podcast-friendly sponsors)

• Gumroad (if selling your own products or templates)

B. Digital Products

• Create a downloadable guide, checklist, or eBook • Mention it in your episodes, link in show notes • Host on Gumroad, Payhip, or Etsy

C. Listener Support

• Platforms like Buy Me a Coffee, Ko-fi, or Patreon • Offer bonus content, shoutouts, or early access for supporters

D. Services

If you're a freelancer, coach, or consultant—your podcast is a portfolio.

Use it to build trust and gently promote what you do.

———

5. Optional: Build a Website or Podcast Hub

Once your show is rolling, you might want a single link to send people to.

Options:

• Podpage – Auto-builds a website from your RSS feed • Carrd – One-page site builder, cheap and clean • Notion + Super – Use a Notion doc as a website with your links, episodes, and resources

This adds professionalism and helps new listeners explore your content in one place.

———

Next up: Chapter 8 — Final Words, Resources, and What to Do Next

Chapter 8: What to Do Next (Keep Showing Up)

Here's the truth nobody talks about:

Your first episode won't be your best.

Your first 10 listeners might just be friends.

Your growth might feel slow at first.

That's all normal. And it doesn't mean you're doing it wrong.

——

What Matters More Than Downloads?

• Consistency — Show up when you say you will • Clarity — Stay true to your message and audience • Connection — Talk like a real person, not a script • Improvement — Just get a little better with each episode

You don't need to sound like NPR or compete with million-download giants.

You just need to carve out your space and stay in it.

——

Keep Things Simple

You don't need to:

• Post every day on 5 platforms

• Book celebrity guests

• Buy expensive gear

You do need to:

• Plan your next episode

• Record regularly

• Share it with people who might care

Let your podcast grow with you.

———

Build a System That Works for You

Start small:

• Batch record two episodes on a Sunday

• Schedule your posts for the week

• Make podcasting part of your routine—not your stress

If you treat it like a job, it'll feel like work.
If you treat it like a creative outlet with purpose, it'll fuel you.

———

You're Already Ahead

Most people never start.

You did.

You've got a show. You've got episodes. You've got something real out there.

Now the only job is to keep showing up and keep hitting record.

You've got this.

Conclusion

Podcasting isn't about having the perfect voice, gear, or setup.

It's about creating space for connection—one episode at a time.

You now have the tools to plan, record, publish, promote, and grow your show—on your own terms, at your own pace.

This isn't about being the loudest in the room.

It's about showing up consistently and honestly, building something that matters.

You're ready. Hit record.

Thanks for Reading

Thank you for trusting Podcast Starter Pack as your launch guide.

If this book helped you get started (or get unstuck), consider leaving a quick review on Amazon—it helps way more than you'd think.

Wishing you clarity, confidence, and creativity with every episode.

Keep showing up. Keep pressing record.

— Mason

About the Author

Mason Wells is a podcast coach, micro-content strategist, and longtime audio storyteller. He helps beginners start and grow simple, sustainable podcasts—without overwhelm or burnout.

When he's not writing step-by-step guides or helping creators fine-tune their message, Mason's either editing indie podcasts, brewing strong coffee, or walking and thinking about what to record next.